Body Language

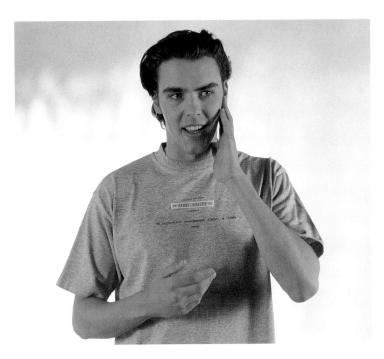

THIS IS A CARLTON BOOK

Text and Design © Carlton Books Limited, 1999

This edition published by Carlton Books Limited, 1999

ISBN 1 85868 774 8

Project Editor: Camilla MacWhannell
Project art direction: Diane Spender
Design and Editorial: Paul Middleton & Neil Williams
Production: Alexia Turner
Picture Research: Catherine Costelloe

Printed and bound in Dubai

Body Language

Easy ways to get the most from your
relationships, work and love life

MARK ASHER

CARLTON

CONTENTS

Introduction

Of all social animals, human beings are the most complex. Much of our body language is instinctive and determined by gender or personality. Some is under conscious control.

OPPOSITE: Appropriate use of body language for self-expression is vital to our social – and consequently our emotional – well-being.

Imagine you are standing on the corner of a busy street in an anonymous city. You are watching the daily hubbub of life pass you by. It is a teeming mass of faces and bodies, a mixture of creeds and colours that blends into uniformity when the eyes are not focused. You begin to focus more on the individuals in the mass, observing their features and characteristics. At once you are struck by the variety of those individuals; the mass has crystallised now into one unique face in the crowd. That face will betray something about the individual, whether it be anger, fatigue, happiness or another emotion.

Nobody has spoken to you and yet you have recognised the paradox that is mankind; we are all similar and yet very different. You have conducted this experiment on the street, at your workplace, at social functions and innumerable other locations before. Often you have passed judgement on the subjects of your observations without realising it. You don't even know these people. Still nobody has spoken to you; you have reached these conclusions by observing the body language they have demonstrated.

We find ourselves in foreign markets, gesturing and pointing at items, dealing with foreign traders. We have no common language and have never met before, yet the trader understands these signs. In a single gesture we dispel the notion that we don't share a common language. We communicate in the most primordial way we know and invariably comprehend one another with the shake of a hand and a nod of the head.

It is this profoundly primordial skill that we very often overlook in our everyday lives. We are genetically imprinted with body language; perhaps it is the very innateness of this heirloom that lets us allow dust to gather upon it. We take it for granted.

More than half of our face-to-face communication is carried out non-verbally. We constantly send out signals, from the clothes we wear to the smiles we wear. We run our hands through our hair, scratch our ears, narrow our eyes, purse our lips. On the surface these may seem mundane, yet if we build up a better understanding of why we do these things, we become more effective communicators. By recognising body language we can also better establish our verbal skills.

This book aims to dust off the common heirloom we all possess but many fail to use properly. Knowledge of body language is not going to change your life, but if you have it you are more than halfway there. In the chapters that follow we discuss the origins of this silent art, the gestures and conflicts, love and respect that emanate from our use of body language.

One by one we will dissect the individual non-verbal signs that we transmit to one another, though it must always be remembered that the language has to be translated as a whole and not by single gestures. We will discuss the origins of the language, how the gestures differ from culture to culture, and how we can use them to motivate ourselves and others, from the bedroom to the boardroom.

1 THE ORIGINS OF BODY LANGUAGE

To comprehend the function of body language we have to examine our evolutionary beginnings and the non-verbal communication that was – and remains – fundamental to our existence as a species. In so doing we acknowledge our shared ancestry with the primates. Despite millions of years apart in terms of evolutionary development, we share a common past.

The World Society for the Protection of Animals recently announced that apes and humans share 97 per cent of their genetic identities and that apes are highly intelligent animals with emotions. They are capable of mental suffering. Furthermore, apes possess distinctive personalities and they form profound emotional attachments with other individuals, just as humans do.

Apes and humans have almost identical brains, and our own intellect is only the result of a proportional increase in size of certain key areas of the brain which control reasoning, intelligence and emotion. In other words, the basic way in which apes and humans think is the same – the processes are just more highly developed in humans.

With regard to expressions, chimpanzees will bare their teeth when excited just as we do, and will shield their faces when frightened. In the hierarchy that exists in the simian world, a subordinate chimp lowers its body much as we would when called before a monarch or celebrity. They are also sufficiently self-aware to use appropriate body language to achieve desired results – for instance a chimpanzee may feign affection and playfulness to cajole favours from another chimpanzee. Even more remarkably, apes and humans share some common innate gestures; for instance rubbing the tummy to signify the message "I'm hungry". They also kiss and embrace to show affection, swagger when proud, chew the ends of their fingers when anxious, and even look longingly into each other's eyes when engaging in mating behaviour.

LEFT: Despite several million years of evolutionary diversity, the basic "blueprint" for apes and humans remains the same. This is only vaguely evident in our physical make-up, but is much more obvious in our facial expressions and body language.

ABOVE: When a chimpanzee focuses on a problem, it will often scratch its head and open its lips slightly, just as we do.

ABOVE: A gorilla in deep contemplation. Such expressions were inherited from a common ancestor of both apes and humans.

Both primates and humans live in social groups in which they seek to reproduce, protect, love and encourage, and interact with others in the group for a wide variety of purposes. The social adaptations of our primate relatives – and indeed the evolutionary adaptations of the animal kingdom as a whole – have left indelible marks on us. Much of the animal kingdom relies to a large degree on body language. We are little different; we merely overlook the importance of it in our lives.

ABOVE: An adult and infant chimpanzee exhibiting social behaviour. Chimpanzees and other primates develop highly complex social relationships and rely on each other not only for physical cooperation but also for emotional bonding.

Body Language through the Ages

The study of body language is still a fairly new science – it is really only in the last century that we have taken a step back to scrutinise our non-verbal communication systems.

Anthropologists have studied mankind in all its diversity. They have made exhaustive investigations into our origins, institutions, religious beliefs and social relationships. Relatively recently they have narrowed some of their efforts into finding out how people communicate with their body actions, and this has resulted in some enlightenment, but also – as in most social research – a minefield of conflicting evidence.

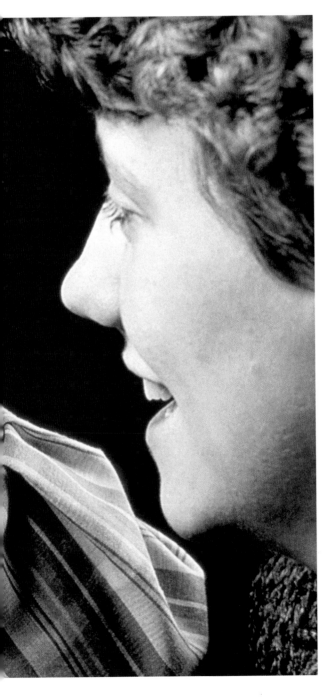

In the fifth century BC Hippocrates discussed human body language and the motivations behind it. Somewhat obliquely he forwarded the notion that our bodies had four basic temperaments which correlated with four body humours, these being phlegmatic, choleric, melancholic and sanguine. His theories on body humours were gradually discredited over the centuries, but his observations are still respected for what they were – a pioneering effort to understand the subject. Hippocrates lived in an era when orators were literally at the centre stage of civilisation, and as communication became an art form the need to understand it became more important.

The great painters of the world, from Titian and Rembrandt to 20th century artists, have made representations of body language and the multiplicity of postures it entails, carefully recording them on canvas for future generations to interpret. From the enigmatic smile on the world's most famous painting, the *Mona Lisa*, to the tortuous works of Francis Bacon, a picture may speak a thousand words, mostly conveyed in extreme subtlety by its subjects' body language.

Consider the indispensable role of body language in the performing arts. The success or failure of an actor's performance depends to an enormous extent on their talent for conveying meaning with their bodies. This was of paramount importance in the days before cinema and television. It was this emphasis on body language that brought us the comic genius of Charlie Chaplin. Chaplin developed his body language to such a degree that he could effortlessly show mannerisms from the pathetic to the comic, bringing the house down with laughter as he did so.

Body language has become specialised to suit many purposes. Bookmakers on race courses have modified body language to display betting odds. Deaf people have developed their own language exclusively based on non-verbal communication.

LEFT: Children reinforce their words with hand signals while their speech is still developing.

ABOVE: Charlie Chaplin was one of the leading exponents of body language in his day; this was particularly so before the "talkies" came into being.

ABOVE: The classic "tick-tack" language used by bookmakers at horse race meetings to pass betting information down the track.

Soldiers have increased their effectiveness and ability to survive on the battlefield by using it to communicate with their comrades.

Some studies of body language were carried out in the seventeenth and eighteenth centuries but it was really only with the emergence of one man's theories in the latter part of the nineteenth century that it became known to a wider audience. Charles Darwin's *The Expression of the Emotions in Man and Animals* (1872) was a landmark achievement. Darwin was fascinated by emotive expressions in blind children and animals. In his book he set out a theory of emotions which recognised that many of our facial expressions were directly inherited from our ape ancestors.

Watergate – Body Language in Action

Throughout history individuals whose talent at body language was paramount are the ones who have left their mark. Likewise those who failed to convey their intended messages through body language have often paid a high price. At the Watergate hearings in 1973 America sat spellbound as one by one members of the Nixon administration perjured themselves on the witness stand. It was plain that many of the administration were lying; even more so when the sound was turned down on the television so that just their body language was there to be observed. One notable perjurer – John M. Mitchell, a high-ranking member of Nixon's staff – repeatedly covered his mouth with his hand after telling lies, or closed his eyes to try to stop his emotions being read.

Manipulative Body Language

Pop stars gyrate their pelvises to bring an element of sexual body language into their performances. On the opposite end of the spectrum, the Pope prostrates himself to demonstrate piousness, knowing that this will be interpreted positively by his followers. Similarly, on a daily basis we see how politicians use a whole range of subtle cues to mould the opinions of the masses.

The sports field is a notable arena not only for acts of physical athleticism and prowess but also as a showcase for displays of body language. What better example might one cite than the pre-match *haka* employed by the All Blacks rugby team? This exhibition of competitive aggression has its roots in the battles of prehistoric Maori societies, but still creates a fearsome impression on the rugby fields of the modern world.

Research has proved the existence of a common, inherited non-verbal ability in all peoples; each and every one of us uses similar facial expressions and gestures to convey our feelings. No matter where we go in the world, humans can communicate with people from other cultures and societies using this innate system, shared by all mankind since we came into existence.

BELOW: The New Zealand **All Blacks** *rugby team demonstrate the* **haka**, *a series of intimidating gestures passed down from ancient Maori societies.*

The Face

Research has shown that women are far better readers of body language than men. They are better at interpreting facial expressions, which may be intrinsically linked to their wider use of them. It has been proved through much research that women smile more frequently than men.

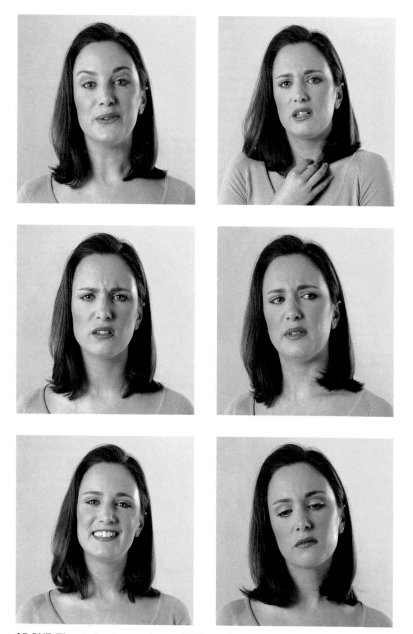

ABOVE: The six basic emotions which can be conveyed by the face (from top left, clockwise): surprise, fear, disgust, sadness, happiness, anger.

Your face is your unique broadcasting device to the outside world, so make sure it conveys what you want it to. Smile and the whole world smiles with you!

There are six basic emotions which can be expressed non-verbally. Let us examine each of them and see how they manifest themselves on our highly dexterous faces.

Surprise When we are surprised, corrugations appear on our foreheads, our eyebrows curve and are raised, our eyes widen, the whites of the eyes become more pronounced and the jaw drops with the teeth parting.

Fear If we are fearful of something, our eyebrows immediately raise and draw themselves together, wrinkles appear in the middle of the forehead, and the eyelids are raised, revealing the whites of the eyes in the process. The facial muscles under the eyes tense up, the mouth opens and the lips draw back.

Disgust When we are disgusted by something our upper lip is raised, our nose wrinkles, the cheek muscles raise and the brow lowers.

Sadness The facial characteristics of sadness include the inner corners of the eyebrows drawing up, triangulation of the skin below the eyelids, quivering lips and in many cases, tears.

Happiness Happiness is generally signified by that most endearing of human facial expressions, the smile. The corners of the lips are drawn back and raised, the teeth are often exposed and wrinkles appear on the outer edges of the eye sockets.

Anger Anger is usually expressed by our eyebrows pulling themselves down, and our eyelids narrowing. Our eyes may become protuberant, our lips clench tightly together and in some cases our nostrils flare.

All this intense visual signalling lends considerable weight to any words we may utter during the course of these emotions. The face conveys our emotions, feelings, attitudes and responses, often on an unconscious level.

Observing Facial Body Language

The next time you are in an audience being addressed by a speaker, make a note of the speaker's facial expressions. Do they convey an aura of sincerity, friendliness, confidence and authority? Or are you reading a face that is flushed, frowning, nervous? Put yourself in the speaker's shoes, up there on that rostrum, looking out on a sea of faces. Would you be apprehensive about addressing the audience? The audience will soon notice if you are. If your audience is smiling, sitting up straight and paying attention, you have positively engaged them. Similarly, if they are not looking at you, if they are fidgeting and their behaviour is generally distracting, you are failing to get your message across.

When you watch the news, observe the facial expressions of the presenter. We associate certain facial expressions with trust or mistrust. The presenters are acutely aware of this and are masters at refining their expressions in order to hold our attention and maintain our respect. Their expressions are as important as their voices.

If the presenter is slumped in the chair, his shoulders rounded, chin dropped into the chest and the eyes fail to maintain contact with us, not only do we have difficulty understanding him, but we also develop doubts about his sincerity, honesty and competence. He has failed to positively engage us. We switch off mentally or change the channel.

Unfortunately, some non-verbal communication is outside our control, since it may in part be conveyed through our physical attributes. For example, we tend to associate certain physical features with certain natures. Bulldog-shaped jaws may be considered as indicative of a tenacious character. The long Roman nose may indicate a patrician quality. Such deductions are usually worthless and totally incorrect – we must always remember to study the entire person and interpret the actual body language being conveyed.

LEFT: Often we convey our emotions through our facial expressions, on an unconscious level, as here when reacting to good or bad news.

BELOW: Eye contact points to a positive interaction here, but her arms across her body illustrate a degree of apprehension.

The Hands

The elaborate way in which we use our hands in conjunction with our speech remains one of the most intrinsic and expressive features in body language. With a single gesture of the hand we give somebody approval, warn them off, even demonstrate our affection for them. The hands are a unique and dazzling language in their own right.

BELOW: The hands are the second most expressive part of our body after the face. They are particularly useful when addressing a large number of people from a distance, such as in teaching.

The hands help us to formulate and elaborate on our verbal communication, and are one of the most animated parts of our body. They are often used to support the spoken word with signals. We have implicit faith in them to reinforce our verbal communication, perhaps even replacing it occasionally when circumstances dictate. Underwater divers have their own sign language, the interpretation of which can mean the difference between life and death, as do soldiers as mentioned earlier. It is extraordinary how much faith we put in our hands.

Have you considered what a crane operator can see from his lofty position? In many cases he requires a banksman – a trained accomplice at ground level – who signals up and down, left or right to direct the safe passage of the goods being moved. Both crane operator and banksman must have complete confidence in each other and the sign language they use in order to avoid disaster. In more subtle forms, the language communicated with our hands can be far more revealing about our nature than we sometimes wish.

Children are often caught telling a lie when their hand automatically comes up to cover their mouth. In adulthood this action remains essentially the same and is easy to spot, especially when allied with other nervous gestures made with the fingers, such as repeated rubbing of the nose and eyes. The subconscious reason for this is to hide as much of the face as possible.

There are many expressions of the hand which are in common usage throughout the world. We are all familiar with the finger drawn across the throat as a statement of being suicidal or doomed; or the imaginary gun made out of fingers and thumb and put to the temple. These very negative signals are easily read.

Positive Hand Language

The thumb is used to make one of the most easily decipherable signals in body language. The raised thumb is almost universally recognised as a positive signal that everything is all right. In a few places, however, it can be a sexual insult. And in a

bar in Germany you may order a beer by sticking your thumb up, whereas if you did the same in Japan you might end up with five beers!

People underline their requests for money by rubbing their thumb against their fingertips.

In the world of cuisine chefs are often witnessed kissing their fingertips as they approve of something. They kiss their fingertips and remove them with a flourish. This gesture of the hand can also demonstrate a man's praise of a woman.

We also use our hands to convey positive messages to others. If we see a performance we admire at a theatre, then we will clap our hands together in appreciation. We may also put our hand out to touch somebody who is either the object of our affection or who is experiencing some personal problem.

Negative Hand Language

We shrug with our palms opened and our arms outstretched to demonstrate indifference or confusion. The "thumbs down" gesture, with the thumbs sometimes jabbed down repeatedly is generally supposed to have come from the Roman gladiatorial arenas and was then an emperor's sign not to save a fallen gladiator's life.

Pinching the nose between thumb and finger states that you think an idea stinks!

A finger that is rotated into the temple is a derogatory form of body language that indicates your opinion that somebody is mad!

Hands clenched together commonly indicates anxiety. The fingers are usually intertwined and held in front of the groin when a person is standing. If seated the fingers adopt the same

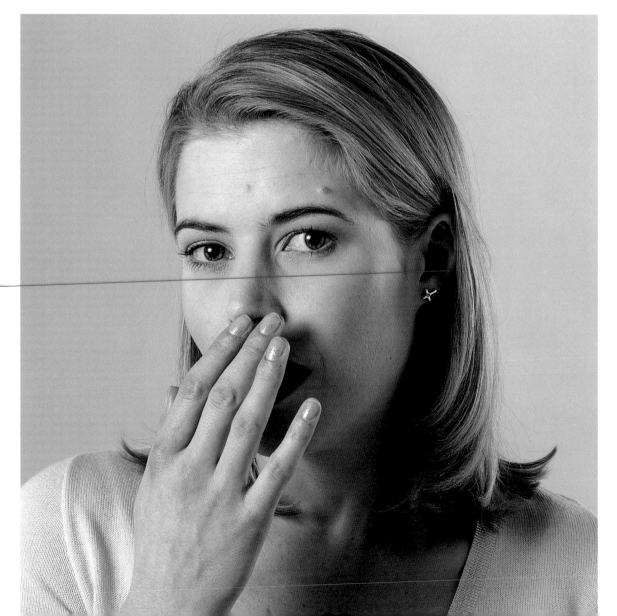

LEFT: *If we are telling a lie we will often cover our mouth with our hand.*

interlocking position and are either clenched in front of the ribcage or raised by the elbows. Each position is a potential barrier to another person attempting to communicate with you. The biting of fingers and fingernails is also commonly perceived as nervous behaviour.

We can often deduce the state of somebody's veracity by their use of their hands and arms. Persistent scratching of the neck, tugging of the ears with the fingers and the apparently innocent stroking of the chin often point to deceiving behaviour, or at the very least body language that fails to support the words being spoken.

Perhaps one of the most offensive signs is the erected middle finger that literally states: "Sit on it."

Others are less obvious. When the hand's first finger and small finger are raised like the horns of an animal, this is an extremely offensive gesture in Italy. It connotes unfaithful women and appears in other Mediterranean countries as a powerful insult.

Another offensive use of the arms and hands is the forearm jerk, where the right arm is bent at the elbow with the left hand rested in the crook of the elbow joint. The right hand is then jerked up in a phallic insult.

The hands are employed in many other gestures – some easily read, some ambiguous. We all react to an angry finger stabbed at us, or a clenched fist raised towards us. In a different scenario that clenched fist may, however, represent a feeling of frustration; equally it may indicate victory. Many of the movements of the hand mean different things when used in conjunction with other body language, so we have to be careful how we interpret them.

Putting our hands in our pockets can often signal feelings of resignation, especially in tandem with a slow walk and a bowed head. If instead we employ a technique with the hands called steepling, we are seen in a better light – here the fingers and thumbs touch to form a church steeple shape: a posture that is indicative of deep contemplation and confidence.

If we put our hands behind our heads we immediately emit signals of confidence, and perhaps a little arrogance. We may point at people to be forceful, rest our head in our hands when boredom strikes, scratch our heads to show confusion, rub our hands quickly together in satisfaction or more slowly when considering something devious and manipulative.

We make obscene signs to each other using our hands, throw them up in submission, greet one another with handshakes and, importantly, touch each other with them. Research has revealed that men are more likely to touch than women; the latter are touched more than men and generally associate the touch with affection and warmth.

The handshake is an interesting facet of human behaviour since it can be done in many ways and convey a whole range of meaning. Sometimes it

BELOW: Cheek touching often betrays signs of surprise or nervousness. A hand that shields the face may also indicate that the person is not being truthful.

can become competitive and the individuals may try to squeeze the resistance out of each other's hands in an attempt to instil acquiescence.

Politicians visiting foreign countries often meet their counterparts with a handshake that borders on the dominant. In many cases the politicians may never have met before, but on virtually every news bulletin one can see them not only grasp the hand but also try and hold the other's forearm with their other hand. This may be taken a stage further as one or even both of them try to grip the other's upper arm or shoulder in conjunction with the handshake.

They are trying to convey with this body language a sense of unity and shared belief.

A less demonstrative use of the handshake is often associated with a dead fish. This is an uninviting and cold handshake with none of the politician's zeal behind it. The hand proffered may often be cold and limp and is in essence like holding on to a dead fish.

Different cultures place different emphases on the handshake. In the Western world – particularly in business practice – it stands as the most recognised form of greeting. The aim of the handshake is to convey feelings of mutual respect and openness between two people. Historically it also demonstrated that you had no weapons to hide! The handshake is a traditional greeting in many parts of the world, although it has variants in different countries. For instance in India and South East Asia two people greeting one another would put their hands together as if in prayer. The French are far more effusive with their handshakes than the British.

Variations on handshakes

When two people meet for the first time they generally shake hands. Northern Europeans in general tend to be less effusive about this pumping action, preferring a solitary movement. Some southern Europeans and many Latin Americans tend to be far more vigorous and pronounced when shaking the hand up and down.

A typical North American variation on the handshake – commonly seen on American basketball and football pitches – involves one person holding his palms open whilst the other slaps his down in appreciation.

Movements of the hands add fluency to all our other body language. You can shut people out of a conversation by a simple dismissive wave, or draw somebody back in with an encouraging open-palmed gesture. The next conversation you have with somebody, make a note of how they use their hands to reinforce their verbal messages. Are they supporting their speech or detracting from it?

ABOVE: The entwined feet may signal an attraction. Her closed hands may however be read as part of a defensive posture.

OPPOSITE ABOVE: A positive sales interaction is taking place here. The salesperson is leaning forward encouragingly, whilst her clients demonstrate their receptiveness with eye contact and open-limbed postures.

OPPOSITE BELOW: It is obvious who the centre of attention is here. The woman on the right is static and tense, whereas the rest of the group are visually more relaxed. Nobody is making an attempt to include her in this social gathering. Time to reassess the situation!

RIGHT: There is harmony between the two couples on the left – broad smiles, open and relaxed postures. The couple on the right, however, exhibit tension with their closed postures and defensive looks.

The Legs

The way we move and position our legs can convey a wide range of attitudes and emotions. Not only does the way we sit or stand offer clues to how we are feeling and our state of mind but it also effects our posture which in turn heightens the impression we put across.

Our legs are vital in giving us the appropriate basic posture. When standing, our posture must be upright if we are not to diminish all our messages to others. Confidence in our deportment is vital to convey that enigmatic feeling we call "presence".

How else, though, do we use our legs in body language? In simplest form, the legs are used to demonstrate openness or defensiveness. An example of this can be seen when a woman crosses her legs; if this is done in conjunction with crossed arms, we may safely presume that she is on the defensive.

However, many men and women sit with their legs crossed in everyday situations and it is thus important to recognise the body's statement in the context in which it manifests itself. The next time you are seated in a large gathering, take note of how many people are sitting with their legs crossed – do they appear defensive, or are they merely sitting in a comfortable position? Clear interpretation must be made before a judgement is derived, or your deductions may be very wrong indeed.

A man who is physically attracted to a woman often displays the most primeval of positions. If he is standing, he invariably points a foot at the object of his desire – in most cases totally unaware that he's

doing this. His legs may be opened, his hands on his hips to emphasise the crotch area. If he is seated, again the foot will be pointing at the woman, but this time the legs may very well be widely extended. Take note of where the woman's feet are pointing.

Similarly, the woman who is attracted to a man may cross one leg over another and subconsciously slip her foot in and out of her shoe in a suggestive fashion. She may twine one foot around the back of the other, which also sends a positive sexual signal. Equally this same act may reveal that the woman is nervous – thus we have to learn to recognise all of the signals and decide on their context before drawing a conclusion.

If somebody is seated and their legs are fully extended, this indicates that the subject is losing interest. Invariably the body will have sunk back, suggesting a withdrawal from any conversation or social interaction that is taking place. A body that shifts its weight backwards and forwards between the two feet transmits a nervous message, as does a body that sways from side to side. Tightly locked legs – particularly when the ankles are locked – indicate a defence mechanism has been triggered. The message is clear – "beware"!

It is useful to glance at the feet momentarily when any social interaction is taking place. If they are pointing directly at you, they are stating unequivocally that the person is interested in communicating with you. If they are pointing to the door, it is very likely that the owner would prefer to be on the other side of that door!

If a person steps back from you, it instantly implies a desire to break away from interaction. They have made a declaration of negative intent with a single step backwards. If you want the conversation to continue, you must take a step forward, or perhaps it would be better to meet later when the person is feeling more receptive.

We need to be aware of walking pace. A measured pace signals assertion and confidence, whereas a stride may well reveal nervousness, an over-confident nature or even aggression!

It may seem a small consideration, but the way you stand can immediately draw someone into communication with you, or shut them out. It may only take a few seconds of forethought preceding an interview or public speaking engagement to decide how you are going to stand or sit to help convey your message.

Deciding how close you are going to stand to someone is vital. Too close and you risk offending somebody, too distant and your sincerity may well be questioned. The most effective stance we can adopt is one that shows us standing erect, but not stiffened. Movements need to be fluid and natural, with the body trunk leaning slightly forward. Resist distracting body language like tapping feet, which may signal impatience, and maintain as much animated fluidity as is appropriate to the situation.

OPPOSITE: The curtsey is performed by someone as a sign of respect when brought before a dignatory. The legs are bent, the head bowed, and the trunk of the body is lowered in submission.

LEFT: Note how the woman's foot is pointing toward the subject of her interest! Members of the group are occupying one another's personal zones, indicating geniality.

The Eyes

Eye contact is an absolutely crucial form of body language. Our eyes reflect the six basic emotions – fear, anger, disgust, surprise, happiness and sadness. We seek eye contact with others when we want to communicate with them, when we are at a distance from them and when we are hostile to them. Equally, by avoiding eye contact we are sending out a variety of negative messages: I am not interested in communicating with you; I dislike you; I am trying to deceive you; I disapprove; I am not attracted to you.

OPPOSITE: An invitation to intimacy. Her looking over her shoulder may only signal friendship at this stage, but it may also be construed as a courting signal in conjunction with her smile and open posture.

Our eyes are a major source of information to others. We give "looks to kill", a "knowing look" and refer in some instances to someone having "bedroom eyes". We can very often get an insight into a person's mood merely by studying their eyes.

Women often maintain their gazes longer than men, and are more likely to make initial eye contact. While eye contact is important for both sexes in most situations, the amount of eye contact we have with someone has to be tailored for every occasion.

Imagine you are being interviewed for a job. You are sitting back in your chair, failing to maintain eye contact with your potential employer. Your eyelids are fluttering and the eyes themselves are rapidly shifting around the room. You are sending all sorts of negative signals. In effect you are saying to that employer, "I'm not comfortable with this situation, or with you, and I don't want to be here". This overrides the positive attitude you are hoping to convey, and can easily have undesirable consequences. The employer has in all likelihood begun a critical evaluation of you, noting any bad posture and your failure to maintain eye contact, and may misinterpret your body language as signifying a bad attitude. You have already been marked down and you haven't even opened your mouth! With a small degree of forethought you could have made sure this situation never arose in the first place.

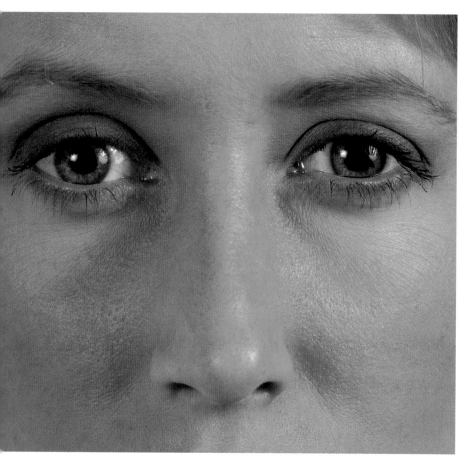

ABOVE: A look of disdain. The pupils are dilating and the eyelids are beginning to narrow. Prolonged eye contact and drawn up eyebrows may indicate anger.

BELOW: The downward glance, the dropped shoulders and the hand in pocket are all symptomatic of someone who is frustrated.

In such situations, it is helpful to tilt the head in conjunction with eye contact. A head that tilts too far forward suggests criticism; similarly a head that is tilted back too far can be seen as trying to convey superiority and may suggest that the subject is staring down his nose. A tilt that conveys alertness and warm interest is obviously best, so an upright, attentive head posture is most appropriate. A sideways glance can send a signal of mistrust. Learn to distinguish between an intimate sideways glance and a suspicious or critical one by scanning all the other body language messages being sent to you.

A rule of thumb is to maintain eye contact for about two-thirds of your exchange with someone else. More, and people find us threatening, less and they think we are not paying attention to them. We basically want to convey the message "I am interested in what you have to say". We can intensify this feeling by nodding occasionally, which transmits further positive messages. In more intimate situations we speak of someone "catching our eye". Our eyes are extremely receptive to the glances of others, and we usually know when someone is watching us – and to a degree, what they are thinking about us. During eye contact, we also subconsciously note how dilated someone's pupils are – the more dilated, the more positive their feelings towards us.

In the work environment, eye contact is an essential skill that both manager and employee need to be aware of and utilise effectively. The manager who shuns intimacy or who prefers to stare out of his window when addressing his subordinates is sending out negative signals to them. This can soon cause problems and misunderstandings. Do not be afraid to look someone in the eye. By doing this you are unequivocally stating that you are ready to talk and listen, and that you are interested.

Blinking

We all blink. It is a natural function designed to protect our sensitive eyes from the glare of sunlight, dust and other airborne hazards. It may be that you wear contact lenses which cause a higher rate of blinking than someone who does not wear them. However, if possible, excessive blinking should be avoided since it can be interpreted as a sign of nervousness or hinder your attempt to convey attentiveness.

If you blink a great deal you tend to block people out. Our normal rate of blinking during a conversation is somewhere between 10 and 20 times per minute. More than that and you may cause the other person to question your integrity and competence. Less, and you may give the impression that you are not taking in what is being said.

Winking

The winking of the eye has a few connotations that have to be observed and deciphered according to the surroundings and events they occur in. The wink is primarily a male gesture although some females will use it too. In Europe and North America it is commonly a signal of complicity. It is also one with a sexual undercurrent – where a man winks admiringly at a woman.

OPPOSITE BELOW: We all know how to catch someone's eye by staring attentively at them. Here the subject may be upset or unhappy and is seeking emotional support or understanding.

LEFT: A raised eyebrow can have many meanings. As in this case, it is often used to convey "a knowing look" or joyful surprise.

2 TERRITORIES

People regard territory and their own space as important and often inviolable aspects of their lives. On the other hand we only have to switch on the television or pick up a newspaper to see territories that have been invaded, violated, even taken over. On a personal level, the amount of space individuals maintain around themselves when dealing with others varies considerably, depending on their culture and the type of social interaction taking place.

n the animal kingdom a bird will sing in order to assert ownership of a nest and the surrounding foliage. A dog will mark his territory by urinating on it, thereby imprinting his scent on his domain.

As human beings our methods may be different, but the basic aim is identical. We put gates in front of our houses and surround the whole with fences, hedges and other physical barriers to endorse the fact that this is our territory. Even within that ring-fenced territory we will take things a stage further and engrave our names on the objects within as a further indication that they are also our belongings!

The next time a door-to-door salesman comes knocking on your door, try to make a point of noting your own territorial behaviour to see how much space you take up in the doorway. You are probably making a statement by spreading yourself as widely across the door as possible, even to the point of leaning from one side across to the other. You are effectively saying "this is my territory".

We demonstrate the ironies of our human natures where territory is concerned; we are very social creatures who thrive on acceptance and intimacy, yet we still feel the need to mark out a

ABOVE: Two men facing each other during a conflict. Here the belligerents invade each other's space – a space that they usually reserve for lovers and friends.

ABOVE: At a social gathering we tend to enter one another's personal zones.

LEFT: As mutual trust increases, a circle forms with each person maintaining an open posture.

BELOW: When we feel threatened our shoulders drop, our gait becomes unsteady and our facial muscles are drawn back.

boundary from which to present ourselves for those acceptances and intimacies. In essence, by creating a territory for ourselves, we have created a world of our own in which to withdraw should anything go wrong. It is a safety buffer zone.

As social as we are, there remain unwritten laws where territory is concerned. For instance we don't usually throw our arms around our boss or indeed any of our other working associates. In these increasingly crowded times territorial behaviour has reached fascinating proportions. Travel on any crowded commuter train in the West and you will see people desperately trying not to touch each other, or even look at each other. We have compromised our very tactile natures in order to maintain our territory.

Space

The physical space we occupy has a great bearing on how we live our lives. It features not only in the buildings and spaces around us but also in flexible spaces such as an office. On entering an office we would generally expect to see a person facing us from behind their desk; or at the very least in profile. With this we are comfortable. We are ready to open conversation and negotiate with this use of space.

If however we turn the desk around and the occupant has his back to us when we enter, we have altered the spatial arrangements. Immediately we find it difficult to converse with the back of the person now facing us. The whole nature of space has been turned on its head and we are confused.

Space is divided into four distinct zones.

LEFT: *This woman is clearly uncomfortable with the man's proximity. Note how her left foot is pointing away from him, conveying her desire to escape from the situation.*

The Public Zone

We all have a public zone which is approximately 12 feet. This would commonly apply to a public speaker or lecturer addressing an audience. Contemporary television broadcasters have attempted to break down this zone by having presenters mingle more closely with their audiences in order to elicit a more personal response from the audience.

The Social Zone

Our social zone is determined in our everyday lives. If for instance a plumber arrives at your home to fix a leaking pipe, you invariably choose a zone between four and 12 feet from him; if you stand looking over his shoulder you are likely to make him feel uncomfortable.

The Personal Zone

In more sociable circumstances we are comfortable to reduce the space between ourselves. This may be anything between 18 and 48 inches and is the type of zone we use for interaction in public places such as bars and restaurants. We do not need to know people particularly well to allow them into our personal zone, but we do need to feel comfortable with them.

The Intimate Zone

Finally, we reserve our intimate zone – from very close up to arm's length – for parents, close relatives, lovers and bosom friends.

In certain cases it is necessary to violate these zones. A doctor carrying out a medical examination may need to breach all four zones to carry out his work properly. A hairdresser must enter our intimate zone if we are to allow our hair to be cut. There is one other visitor that we allow into this zone without feeling our space is being invaded – our domestic pet.

Appropriate use of space is an essential part of our daily lives. Too little of it and we have no 'breathing space', too much of it and we feel abandoned and isolated. We have unfortunately written ourselves a set of commandments which are difficult to adhere to where space is concerned. We must not touch, we must not get too close, we must maintain our distance. This is rather astonishing for such a tactile creature as the human being.

Cultural Uses of Space

In many cultures it is everyday behaviour to engage in physical contact with other people, even of the same sex. Some Europeans are more relaxed about spatial distances than others. Continental Europeans meeting a stranger tend to be far more open-minded in their use of space than the British, who are notoriously reserved. Thus it is important to recognise that space is culturally determined.

In an Eastern country it can be construed as offensive behaviour not to kiss a member of the same sex when meeting. In this case not only has the intimate zone been crossed by a relative stranger, but they have been allowed to kiss a member of the same sex. If this occurred in Britain or the United States, it could well give rise to questions about the sexuality of these two men.

Inhibitions

Space does present us with rather a dilemma, though. We all require a space to work in, to breathe in, to love in and in which to express ourselves. If we crowd someone we can make them feel uncomfortable. They step back from us, their shoulders are stiff, they are frowning, the arms are crossed and their body turns away from us. We have just been told that we are not welcome in this space.

There are no definitive rules where space is concerned. We allow a different space to come between ourselves and a lover and ourselves and our employer, and the choice of space is determined both by culture and by individual preference.

Observe how genders use space differently. In public we are often presented with scenes of women side by side, holding each other, hugging each other. Men reserve a larger space between themselves than women and are not so intimate.

ABOVE: In many cultures, conversation may be comfortably pursued even in very close proximity.

OPPOSITE: Here we see how eye contact, relaxed posture, and feet pointing toward each other create positive body language and aid successful interaction.

Body Pointing

Body pointing is one of the less obvious components of body language. We do it so automatically that we are often unaware of it and how it might be affecting us. If for instance two men are having an argument they may point their bodies away from each other at an angle to emphasise their disagreement. Their hands will very likely be resting on their hips, their arms forming a triangle. If this is to proceed to direct confrontation then they will front each other up and stand squarely facing each other. These are automatic gestures.

RIGHT: The head shrinking into raised shoulders is often a sign of nervousness and worry.

LEFT: Women find intimacy with each other easier than men do, and this is reflected in their body language.

I n more positive surroundings you can present a more open and accessible self by adopting less relaxed positions of the body that hinder your communication. By opening your stance and maintaining eye contact you will be surprised at how much easier communication is.

Next time you are in conversation with two or more people make a note of where your body is pointing. Make a quick mental note of how each person is standing in relation to you. Do you feel shut out of the conversation? Or are you all maintaining open body stances that allow you to feel drawn into the conversation?

What does it tell you if somebody you are speaking with has his body pointing away from you? By itself it may just mean that they are also trying to talk to somebody else on the opposite side. Look for clusters of signals. If the person is yawning, looking at the floor, scratching and generally distracted then the likelihood is that you have not got his full attention.

When we are seated for any amount of time we will invariably cross our legs. We discussed earlier how this can send a negative message to our opposite number. If you want to cross your legs then try and point a knee and foot at the other person.

You are signalling to the other person that you accept a situation and maintain an interest in it.

Take the scenario of an attractive woman being spoken to by an admiring man. Another man arrives in the area. The first man will immediately try and shut out this new rival by pointing his body more directly at the woman and thereby excluding the competitor. This certainly makes it harder for the newcomer to interact in the couple's territory.

LEFT: This person looks uneasy. Her shoulders are at an uneven level and she is clutching her knee suggesting that she is unsure about something.

In Public

Try watching people at work, at home, on a train. How do they "point" their bodies? When we build up a rapport with somebody we often imitate their body language subconsciously. At other times we deliberately copy somebody's actions to give them a positive feeling about themselves. Be aware that you are doing this, or not, as the case might be.

You can influence the way a conversation goes by paying attention to where you are pointing. If you want to appear more open and interested then concentrate on where you point yourself, the space you use, your facial expressions, the use of your hands and the other elements of body language.

Overall, make sure your body language is in harmony with your speech. It may all sound a bit stiff and formalised but body-pointing at a person is actually one of the most natural positions you can adopt.

Resist movements such as swaying from side to side or rocking backwards and forwards. Instead, try to exhibit a more steady stance, but not too statuesque.

When Abroad

In foreign countries it is always advisable to observe the body language and learn from it, particularly in less liberal countries. Watch how local people use space, body pointing and other features in their body language. At what distance from another person is it usual to stand in this culture? Should you look people in the eye throughout a conversation? It is important that you use and respect local mannerisms.

RIGHT: Different degrees of body pointing shown in this picture convey clues about each individual's level of comfort with the person nearest to them.

OPPOSITE: Signs of conflict here, from the prolonged eye contact to the deliberate pointing of each body away from the other.

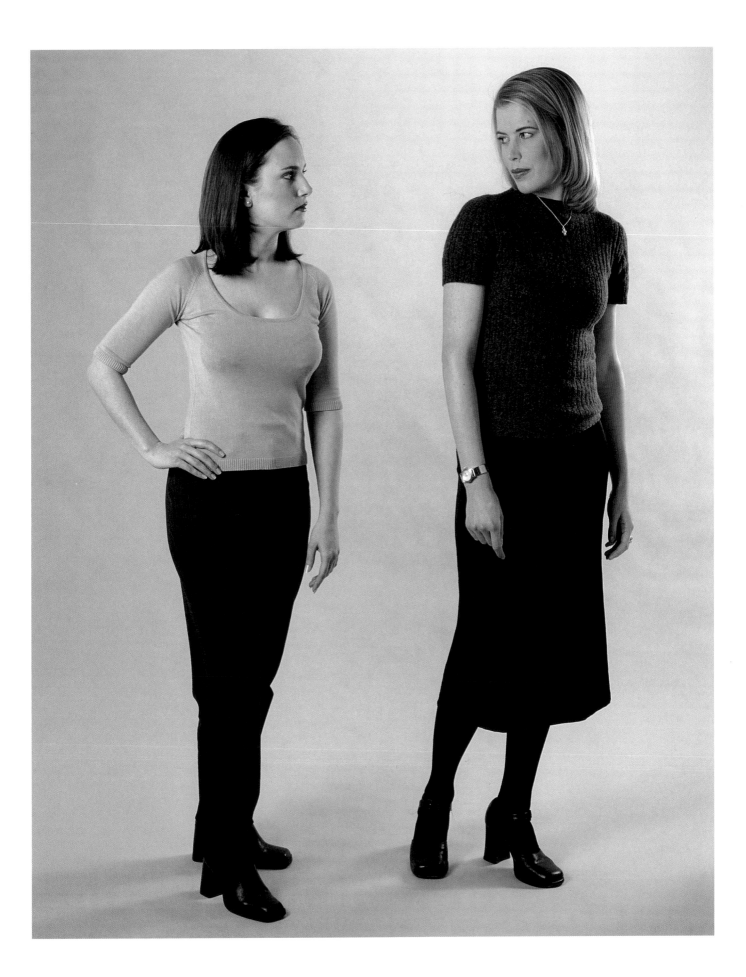

Gestures

What are gestures? In short, actions that speak louder than words. A gesture is an act that conveys our emotions. They are conveyers of all sorts of information not easily expressed in verbal language.

The world of gestures is enormous and it would be quite impossible to cover them all here. We shall stick to ones in common usage and explain how they support our verbal language.

Ridicule

Slapping the forehead is a gesture of self-ridicule and is frequently made when we have forgotten something. In parts of Europe – notably Germany – a person who has tired of another's conversation will often cup his hand by his chest, indicating he could have grown a beard in the time it has taken the other to get his point across! In South America, a person who strokes their ring finger up and down their throat is implying that what you are saying is nonsense!

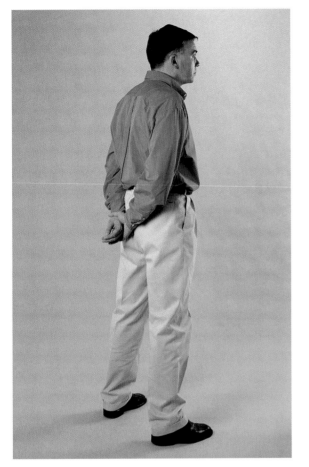

ABOVE: A military officer will use this type of stance to convey his authority, superiority and even disdain.

ABOVE: Arms folded with an upright stance is easily interpreted as unequivocal confidence.

The Arms Raised

The raised arm has several meanings. Commonly used in the classroom to attract attention, it is also used to signal a halt to something and when swearing an oath in court. When both arms are raised it can mean 'I surrender' or 'I am triumphant'.

Hidden Signals

Where the arms are tucked behind the back and the hands are clasped together we can generally accept that somebody is comfortable with a situation, although we may still find it suspicious that they are hiding their hands from us.

Barriers

When the arms are brought to the front this becomes a method of blocking people out. The brushing of the cheeks with the backs of the fingers indicates boredom and uncertainty. When we puff up our cheeks we are essentially saying that something or someone is fat! A jutting out chin suggests hostility. A person we see fiddling with their cuffs is exhibiting nervous behaviour. Someone rubbing their eyes may be trying to deceive you – but note that the person may simply be tired.

Where a hand is clenched into a fist and the other comes down on top of it repeatedly with an open palm, we are telling someone "screw you" or "I got screwed".

On a military parade ground an officer will often be seen walking up and down, the palm of one hand tucked inside the other behind his back. He is making an assertive statement here: "I am confident and superior." There are however small differences when the hands are clasped behind the back. If the hand is holding the wrist this states that the person is nervous. As the hand progresses up the arm it amplifies that state of nervousness.

OPPOSITE RIGHT: The "triumphant" gesture, with the arms raised above the head, is even older than the human species.

Reading the Language

Watch for acts of complicity between two people. A person tapping his nose is signalling that he wants to keep things under wraps from others. Similarly the wink of the eye generates much the same message.

The poking out of the tongue is a childhood gesture that we carry over into adulthood. It is even used in the primate world, so must be one of our most ancient and innate gestures.

If somebody is rubbing their ears when you are talking to them you are unlikely to have their full attention. They are in effect saying 'I've heard enough of this'. Again when we scratch our necks we are transmitting signals of doubt. We support our chins in our hands and immediately send a message of boredom. Curiously, the hand may only have to move slightly away from that position and touch the cheek to generate an entirely different message: "I am now interested."

Feel assured when someone is scratching their chin; they are evaluating something prior to making a decision. Feel less assured when somebody you are talking to is fiddling with their watch. They are telling you they are impatient. A shoulder shrug can be seen in the same light. It is a signal of resignation, uncertainty and the prelude to an early departure! When the hand starts retreating behind the head, holding the neck or head with the palms open we should see this as a signal of conflict and disagreement. Athletes and children are observed to put their hands behind their heads when cross or disappointed. Try to make a point of reading these signs as they appear and you will find it will complement the rest of your communication and powers of interpretation.

OPPOSITE: We let our guard down completely when confiding in someone. As this couple share a joke, note how the man raises his elbows and leans forward slightly for increased intimacy, while the woman points her hands and face towards him.

FAR RIGHT: A wagging finger has a demotivating effect. His hand hooked into the belt suggests a sense of superiority of opinion over hers. Tension is visible in her face, and note how she is rubbing her finger with apprehension.

RIGHT: The "thumbs up" for many of us sends a clear message that everything is fine. In certain parts of the world however it can be interpreted as a sexual insult.

Posture

What exactly does our posture say about us? In short it projects a message to others of our future intent. We all want to project a more positive image of ourselves and one way in which we can do this is by correcting our posture. By adopting a better posture we give the world a better picture of ourselves. Posture is then a reflection of the way we see ourselves and the way we want others to perceive us. It is a wordless statement on our outlook on life, sent out to all those around us.

Poor posture can signal a lack of self-esteem. A person who is hunched up, head down, eyes to the ground, round shouldered and with splayed feet is hardly likely to galvanise our attention for long. We immediately pick up messages of shame, humility and withdrawal. Conversely, a person who stands up straight and walks tall captures our attention far more. Here is a character displaying an interest in his surroundings and the people around him.

We have probably all been in the situation where a person's posture and bearing has told us that they are not interested in us. Or we ourselves have adopted a defensive posture when in the company of somebody unfamiliar to us. Postures and gestures often let us know how a person is feeling. We all know how a tramp feels by his slumped posture and eyes half-closed in resignation. Similarly another person will quickly pick up on our negative body language when we are feeling low or depressed.

A good posture is one that draws a vertical line down from the ears through the shoulders, the lower back curved inward slightly and the head held up. When you try this at first it may be uncomfortable but this is because many of us unconsciously slouch. A perfect example of posture can be found on the fashion catwalks where the models have perfected a feline grace coupled with an appealing posture, the result of which is a rhythmic and fluid set of body movements.

We can determine a person's resolve to deal with a tricky problem by noting their posture amongst the other cluster of body language signals. Is the body pointing away from the problem or facing up to it? Does the person look ready to tackle the task? Not if the shoulders have dropped and the chin sunk. Is the person erect to the point that they look statuesque? If so they are probably more than a little daunted by the idea. Much research has shown that our value, judgement and liking of a person can be greatly influenced by the posture they assume.

Breathing exercises can help to improve your posture as the two are intrinsically linked. If the shoulders are dropped and the chin has sunk into the chest then more weight is transferred to the ribcage. All these movements can and do rapidly reduce the projection of your voice and the ease of your breathing.

Our postures change as we shift weight from one foot to another. Therefore if we shift backwards and forwards we make ourselves look cunning – giving the impression that we are trying to wriggle out of the situation we find ourselves in.

OPPOSITE: The French sculptor Auguste Rodin portrayed an instantly recognisable image of body language – deep thought.

In everyday life the happiest and most successful people we see around us maintain good postures. Politicians go out of their way to look upright because it projects a positive impression. The stars of screen and stage also adopt many different postures in order to portray their characters to us. Bouncers on nightclub doors puff themselves up in order to demonstrate strength. Diplomats assume postures that convey a message of conciliation blended with resolve, even before they have entered into any negotiations. Posture is a fundamental facet of body language, and needs to be used in conjunction with other non-verbal language to create the desired impression.

RIGHT: Her slumped posture and downward stare both signal resignation. If she was to adopt this posture at an interview the likelihood of her succeeding would be remote.

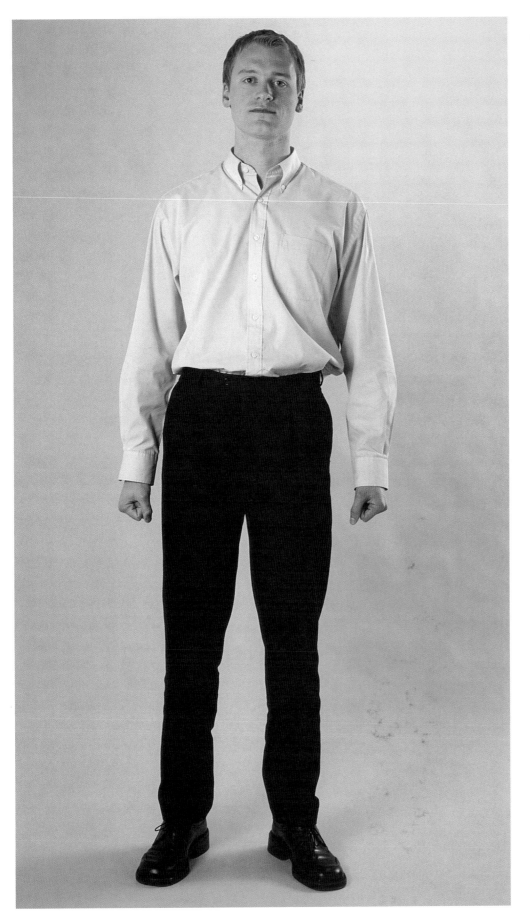

LEFT: An erect posture can convey attentiveness, but if as here it is too stiff it can look threatening and tense.

Assertion

All the various forms of body language discussed thus far can be combined appropriately to create an aura of confidence and competence – an attitude of assertion. It is perhaps one of the easiest things in the world not to be assertive. It requires only a lack of eye contact, a few nervous facial expressions, some hand wringing, dropped shoulders and a defensive posture and the impression is complete. The damage is done, and we have stated our case weakly to an employer, a colleague or a prospective lover.

RIGHT: This manager should really have approached his secretary from the front of the desk, thereby making conversation easier and more relaxed. At least there is a degree of space for manoeuvring should they fall into a discussion.

OPPOSITE: The situation has become intolerable here, however. It can be very disconcerting to have someone of higher authority look over your shoulder when you are working. The woman will now struggle to assert her opinion if work is discussed.

Assertion springs from the need to put forward your own ideas and thoughts, respecting others you come into contact with but ensuring you put yourself over to them in a strong, confident manner.

So how do we make ourselves more assertive? For a start, don't make yourself into somebody you are not. When describing your feelings use first person statements: "I feel that...", "I want you to know that...". These are direct statements that can't be mistaken for anything else and leave the opposite party in no doubt as to your intentions and your determination to achieve them.

Avoid being aggressive in your demands at all costs. We have to find the platform between aggression and submission. This balance has to include taking a stance on something, believing in it and putting forward proposals that will bring it to fruition.

To avoid being submissive we need to cut out long rambling statements and the frequent justifications that come with them. Do not put yourself down under any circumstances. Avoid dismissive statements like "It doesn't matter". It is all too easy to fall into the trap of becoming aggressive, too, especially when things are not

BELOW: These women are distinctly ill at ease, making eye contact from a sideways glance rather than face-to-face. Perhaps mutual mistrust is hampering their ability to convey confident assertion.

going our way. This is counter-productive and usually ends up with other people's negative opinions of you being regarded as cast iron facts. Assertion comes by way of using smiles, open palms, and an understanding of space; if we stand too far away then our objectives remain distant.

We can all recall a situation that we entered expecting A, B and C and came away without any of them. We were afraid to stand up for ourselves and yet if we had, the same people would have respected us more for it. Try to be less self-conscious about how other people see you; get yourself noticed and don't submit in every situation that arises. Remember assertion happens today, not tomorrow. In the event of a setback, reason out a new approach and reassert yourself. Be tenacious and straightforward in your demands, but never intimidate.

Couple this all with a steady gaze, a middle range tone of voice and open facial expressions and posture. Be aware of your speech delivery and breathing rate as these may affect your level of assertion.

If you can't meet your objectives head on then offer to compromise. If you are subjected to criticism then stand your ground. The worst possible thing to do is to emulate bad behaviour.

Don't sell yourself short or threaten others when asserting yourself. Use open-ended questions that will require a response from the other person: 'Am I making making myself clear here?'

Assertion is needed in all aspects of life from dealing with your children and lover, to an intransigent member in your workplace. Remember too the continuous nature of body language. You are constantly sending out signals to everybody around you, and if those signals are weak then you have a mountain to climb. Try to be more consistent yourself and you will see that others' perception of you will soon change for the better. You will be seen in a new light. Don't forget that body language used well is a statement that indicates your power and status in life. Keep your facial expressions mobile and emphasise key words in stating your objectives. When asserting yourself keep an eye on the other person's body language. What does it tell you? Are they responsive to your assertions or are they backing off? Do you need to consider using another strategy? The true test of asserting yourself is found in the results that come from it. You will feel far more positive about yourself and others when you have achieved that objective.

BELOW: The working environment here seems to be relaxed, with these individuals at ease in each other's company. Their posture is open and friendly and is reflected in their direct eye contact and facial expressions.

Conflict

We need to be balanced and rational about how we approach conflict and how we disarm it. Rarely if at all do raised voices and highly charged displays of body language result in a satisfactory conclusion to a conflict, personal or otherwise.

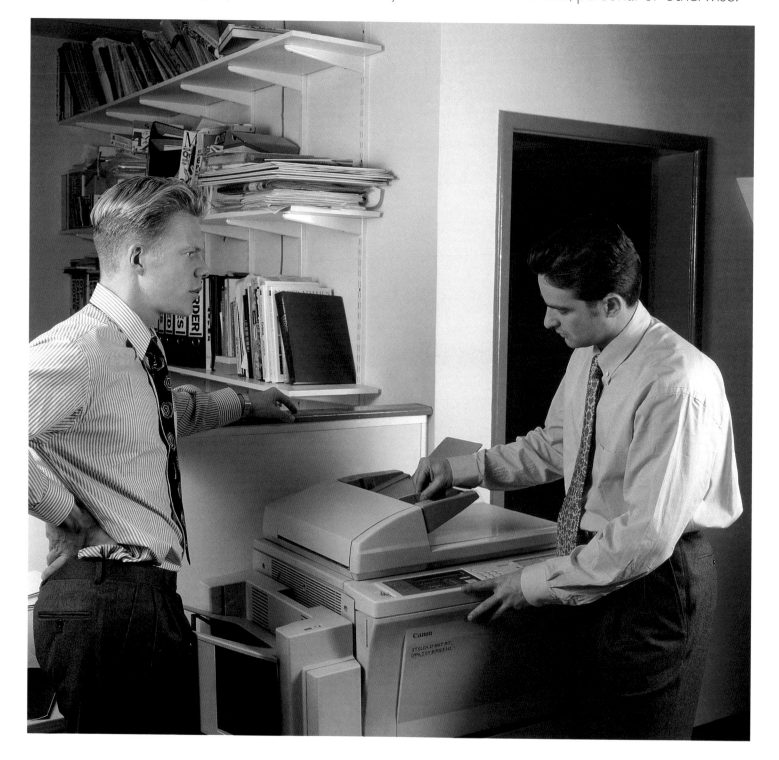

Conflict arises in many areas of our lives. It is a normal human reaction to something that goes against our own personal wishes.

Recognising conflict and its origins is the perceptive way to deal with it. Look for the lowered head, the closed posture, the locked limbs, the sideways glances, furrowed brow and lowered eyebrows; all are signs that indicate the person is feeling critical towards you. As conflict worsens then the body language may start to become more animated and abusive. The eyes may be looking down the nose now, a single finger or the "V" sign may be used. From there on it is a downward spiral of threats and bad feeling. Confrontation is one of the most unsatisfactory results of conflict. It seeks only to further antagonise another person or situation. The banging of the fists on a desk might get your point heard but it will ultimately have a demotivating effect on the other person.

How do we go about defusing this potential time bomb in front of us? One thing you might consider is lowering your body. When we feel threatened we often make ourselves appear smaller to diminish the threat. This is a recognised way of reducing conflict. Open the palms of your hands to show you are not a threat to the other person. Most important, stop talking or shouting at the other person. You can't possibly hope to listen to another's viewpoint if you continue talking. Keep trying to develop a permissive attitude and keep listening. Patience is of paramount importance in these situations. Don't lose your temper. You might win the conflict but ultimately you lose the war! Ask questions that encourage the other person. Be specific in your demands but don't be complacent about them.

OPPOSITE: Trouble is brewing here. The prolonged eye contact – in the nature of a challenge – from the man on the left is dismissed by the other man as he seeks to go about his business.

LEFT: A defensive tilt of the head and the corrugations on the forehead indicate embarrassment. In a conflict situation, people will try to hide such expressions of self-doubt since it sends the message: "You have won."

You will need a good deal of assertion and diplomacy to bring a conflict to a mutually agreeable standstill. If you become aggressive you are likely to overstate your case, exaggerate, become irrational, begin denigrating the other person's viewpoint and constantly interrupt. As the process deteriorates then blame will start to be apportioned, character assassination will begin and truths will suddenly become intolerably stretched to the point where they are blatant lies. Shouting and screaming may very well then descend into physical threats.

To deal with a conflict in an assertive manner your objectives have to remain clear at all times.

You have to establish the other's viewpoint and then try to seek out common ground. If you reach an impasse whereby neither of you can reach any common ground then try and smooth things over and return to it when you can both give a better and more rational account of yourselves.

Conflict often arises in the home. Teenagers suddenly find that the previously unchallenged set of parental rules is now up for reappraisal. This often results in conflict. Try to look for changes in the child's behaviour and attitudes. Look for the signs of obstructive body language. In some cases you may be able to talk things through before a conflict arises.

3 EFFECTIVE USE OF BODY LANGUAGE

Consider what would happen if body language was removed from your repertoire for the day. Ask yourself what it would be like to try to communicate without the use of all those gestures, hand signals, frowns, scowls and smiles. How difficult would it be to get your message across with your arms tied behind your back and your face set in stone?

How would we magnify our feelings of happiness, doubt, sincerity? In short we couldn't. We rely upon our body language to support our speech. Without it speech just becomes a dull monologue.

Daily life demands all manner of body language. Entire professions would be rendered quite useless by the removal of their body language. Cricket umpires would become obsolete, as would opera singers and film actors. Even the traditional market trader would be reduced to a sedentary status. What would the result be for the artist and sculptor if his model just sat rigidly exhibiting no body language? How would the bookies get their messages across?

The spoken word loses most of its impact in the absence of the accompanying gestures and postures. This loss of spontaneity reduces us to talking automatons. We need to be able to reinforce our words, even contradict others' words by use of our body language. Our ability to greet somebody or even ignore them is triggered in the first instance by a bodily response.

Think of your favourite film, and imagine it with all the body language removed. However adept and incisive the dialogue we would sooner or later find the whole thing repetitious. The rhythm and resonance of the language might still come across, but the continuity and atmosphere would have gone.

ABOVE: A spontaneous kiss on the doorstep before the day begins reassures this couple that their relationship is both stable and successful.

ABOVE: Gestures are another way of communicating one's feelings, to reinforce a bond of trust and security.

In many situations we need to reach out and touch something or somebody to underpin our speech. No amount of words can convey admiration like the common touch can.

A simple exercise in understanding how profoundly body language affects us is to think about a recent conversation with someone. You may recall little or none of the actual conversation you had with them but you will undoubtedly recall some of their body language. This underlines the fact that non-verbal cues are more important to us than spoken language.

LEFT: His body is withdrawn and slumped showing frustration in contrast to her confident, open and helpful manner.

BELOW: This social interaction has become a positive one as far as each couple is concerned; note however how they have "paired" off, blocking a collective interaction.

Body Language in the Workplace

It is desirable for us to use appropriate body language in our social life, but it is absolutely vital that we do so in the workplace. Our livelihood and status in life may well depend on it.

The World of Corporate Sales – a Crucial Arena

Marketplaces have become increasingly crowded and profit margins squeezed as a result. Thus many sales divisions and companies have taken a serious look in the mirror at themselves to see what image they project. Many Japanese companies pioneered this sort of self-examination and it resulted in an overhaul of their business philosophies. The image that individuals project is of huge importance, and body language is by far the biggest component in the projection of image, competence and charisma.

Success and Climbing the Corporate Ladder

Even in a non-sales environment, body language is important. There may be wide chasms between you and your colleagues in terms of pay, conditions, aspirations and the way you conduct workplace relationships. Pick out the most successful people in your workplace and try to evaluate their body language and mannerisms. Watch how they plan and delegate work efficiently, treating people on all levels evenhandedly. Pick out all the positive and negative points that you can see and apply them to yourself. Look at your colleagues' use of space and how they mark their territory. What does their appearance say about them? What does yours say about you?

How did some of them get promoted over you? You have said and done all the right things in the past but your face just didn't seem to fit. Are you as approachable and amenable as them? Why do they look so much more confident and assertive than you? The answer could very well lie in your poor use of body language, your failure to look your boss in the eye, and your lack of personal confidence.

Breaking Down the Barriers

Both employer and employees need to recognise the importance of body language in the workplace. Thus we need to encourage better and more open working relationships with one another, with minimal stress and discomfort.

How Body Language Affects the Outcome of Job Interviews

We have to drive ourselves increasingly today as the workplace has become more and more competitive. The alternative is unemployment or an undesirable occupation. We return again to the subject of assertion.

OPPOSITE: The couple shaking hands are generating a positive response to each other with a firm handshake, eye contact and smiles. However the salesman in the foreground is showing signs of being under pressure with his tight and immobile posture and his stern facial expression.

Even before we began work we needed to assert our authority in order to get an initial interview. We needed to sell the idea that we were good for the company. We sent a letter of application and waited for the next post. Eventually we were granted an interview. But this is not the end of our struggle – in many ways it is where the demands really begin.

The interview is a social interaction with a clearly defined purpose. In many cases it will be our only chance to demonstrate we are "up for the job"; that we have the abilities and talents to carry out the tasks, and that we like the environment and company. Both employer and potential employee should be looking for clear messages from each other as the interview progresses. An interviewer will have made a large number of judgements about you within the first five minutes. You need to maximise the clarity of your positive signals right throughout the interview. What unfortunately is more common is that we arrive totally unprepared and make a mess of the whole interview.

RIGHT: A positive attitude and "open" gestures here will do much to secure her a successful outcome to this job interview. Note the use of "power seating", where the interviewer has set herself proportionately above the interviewee with a higher chair.

Reading the Signals

To avoid this situation we should have travelled to the place of interview and taken some minutes to absorb all the information around us. We should have looked at the body of physical evidence around us. How did the security guard react to us when we arrived? Was he indifferent or was he interested? Does his attitude alone begin to tell us anything about the company inside? Look at the workplace itself and the location. Try to form initial impressions of the company, developing opinions about it.

RIGHT: A "couldn't care less" attitude is demonstrated here. Whilst the hands might be in the pockets for comfort, the dismissive over the shoulder look and attached scowl say it all about his mood!

A Negative Scenario

Is the building dirty, the garden overgrown, with litter everywhere? Perhaps the managing director's car is parked in a space far removed from the rest of the workforce's. If so, you could safely draw the conclusion that a strict hierarchy exists here, with a great deal of dissatisfaction. Might this be echoed inside the workplace walls? Would you be happy to work in such an environment? You can make these sort of informed conclusions to draw up your own image and see how it matches the one that emerges from the actual interview.

You walk into the building and take note of the use of space. Even the arrangement of office furniture works a little like body language.

You introduce yourself to the receptionist who fails to even look up and make eye contact. Whilst it would be unfair to tar everyone in the building with the same brush, you are beginning to get a negative feel for the place and your enthusiasm is rapidly on the wane. Unconsciously, you are pointing your feet towards the exit. The interview is conducted in a smoke-filled room where the employer has his feet on the desk or over his chair. He is unequivocally stating "this is my territory".

You can't see his hands behind the table and yet he can see yours as you pick minute pieces of fluff from your clothing. You have just given out a piece of negative body language and he will have noticed it.

OPPOSITE: An awkward display of body language as the lip curls down and the eyes narrow. She is tentative and very unsure of herself.

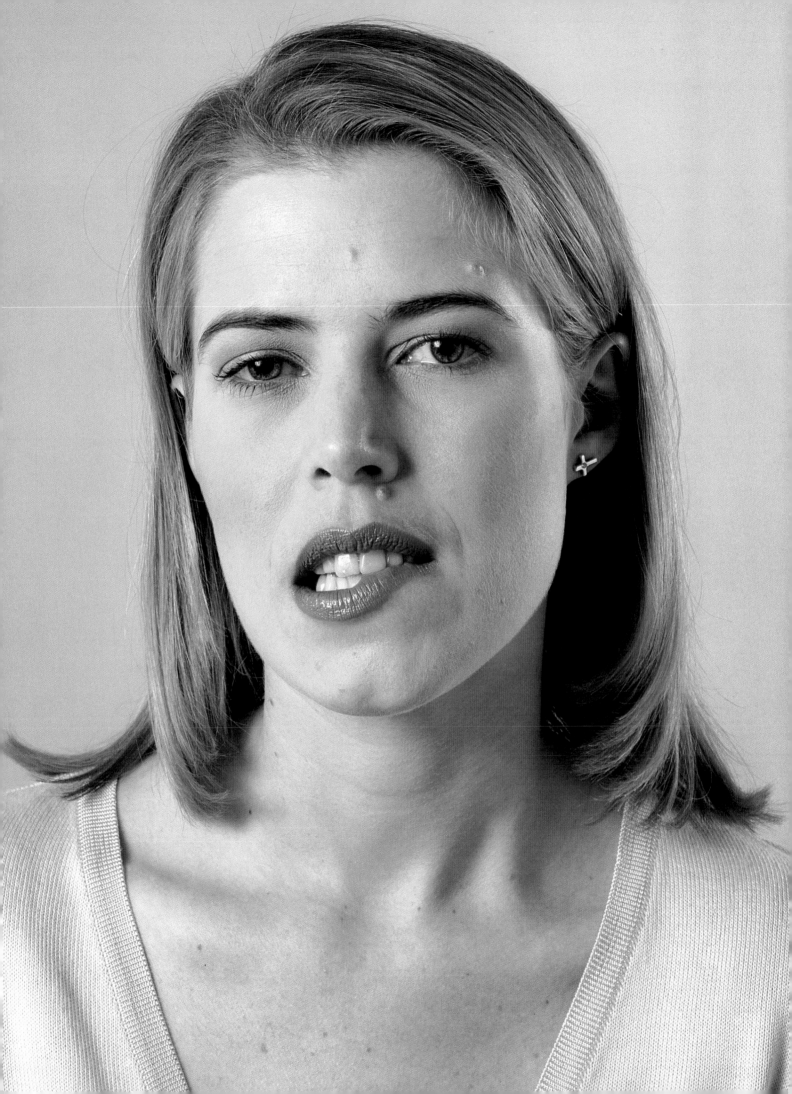

BELOW: *Hair pulling or "tugging" is associated with feelings of frustration, whereas twining curls around fingers and "toying" with the hair often has a sexual connotation.*

His handshake will assume the proportions of his ego; thus he will probably squeeze the life out your hand. He may even try to dominate you further by having his seat raised slightly so that he towers above you. Perhaps his face reflects a stiff formality; a lack of geniality that affirms his wish to convey an air of superiority. This is a boss who clearly regiments his workforce through force of personality. Are you happy to fit into this sort of regime? How will you alter your body language to meet this challenge to your self-confidence?

Inevitably aggression will meet aggression. He will probably do little to hide his, whereas you, out of respect, will quietly seethe in your chair until the "interrogation" is over. You sit stiffly forgetting about things like appropriate posture and maintaining eye contact. You end up looking right through him and not really hearing what he

has to say. He fires questions at you rather than asks them, interrupts you when you try to answer. His speech is very "I" oriented. He drums his fingers impatiently on the table as he waits for your answer. He stares at you dominantly from his position some feet away. A subordinate employee comes in with a single cup of tea, smiling at you timidly. There is only one cup of tea in the room – and only one ego.

You clearly are going to be a very little fish in this man's pool. His aggressive outlook and obstructive body language has shown that.

This is a man who belittles what you say, dismissing it with a cursory wave of the hand. You find him threatening and your body is upright in the chair, exhibiting your discomfort. Your breathing pattern has become one of short nervous breaths which in turn affect the tone of your voice and speech delivery. You find it impossible to display positive body language, and the communication process diminishes to the point of ineffectiveness. At the end of the interview you feel you have been through an ordeal. There can be only two possible outcomes from this interview: either you are offered a job in a tyrannical environment, or the body language you have shown the employer has scuppered your chances of a job offer anyway. A positive outcome is clearly impossible under such circumstances.

BELOW: This meeting is working very well, with all eyes on the speaker. He has an open posture and is easy with his hand movements, which results in a confident manner.

A Positive Scenario

Fortunately you have another interview the following day. Again you are nervous but you have taken time to compose yourself and check your breathing.

You arrive for the interview. This time the building is open plan, the gardens are well-tended, and there are no physical barriers. The receptionist smiles warmly as you introduce yourself. Her body posture is upright but relaxed. She has an open stance and maintains eye contact with you. She makes you feel comfortable, which in turn makes her a good advertisement for the company. You are shown to a room where the boss stands up and walks around his office desk to shake your hand. He has recognised the desk's potential as a barrier to geniality. He shakes your hand, introduces himself and smiles. You sit down feeling far more relaxed than you were the day before. Without realising it you are drawn into his positive body language. He is attentive, open-palmed and receptive.

As you confer both of you remain in an open-armed position, which immediately makes you both more accessible. If your hands were to suddenly drop beneath the table your potential employer would probably be momentarily uncomfortable. He would wonder what he had done wrong to put you on your guard.

OPPOSITE: Despite their bodies being "closed" to each other, the smiles and looks over the shoulder point towards positive interaction. This could possibly mean a successful outcome to an interview, or a good appraisal.

RIGHT: This meeting has begun in a very positive way. Both parties seem at ease and confident enough to step into each other's territory without a second thought. Eye contact is strong and the smiles are genuine, reflecting mutual respect.

You relax. He begins to gauge your opinions, thoughts, motives, ambitions and ideals. He is easy-going and yet assertive. He nods his head and encourages you further. Your breathing pattern is regular and you give a far better impression of yourself than on the previous day. Much of this is in reaction to the positive body language the interviewer has been broadcasting to you. The friendliness conveyed through positive body language is contagious, and you are already forming a positive relationship. The outlook for you is good, as is the potential for you to succeed

if this company takes you on.

In many successful companies today the managers have paid great attention to positively engaging themselves with the rest of the workforce. They further concentrate on how they handle employees on an everyday basis. They are clear and concise with their instructions and encourage the use of open-ended questions, e.g. "How do you feel about this project?", which in turn actively involves the employees in the decision-making process. They give praise where praise is due. In the event that criticism has to be made, accusing fingers and table-thumping do not figure in the process. Criticism is constructive, and care is taken to use it without demotivating or demoralising the person on the receiving end. Body language is positive in order to cultivate trust, empathy and understanding. This contributes significantly to a pleasant and optimistic attitude amongst employees, and a better work environment.

Good managers build up a rapport with their workforce which is reflected in productivity and corporate success. They take a note of the environment, the noise, the lighting, even the arrangement of furniture.

This may all seem a far cry from the world of facial expressions and other components of body language, but the utilization of space in buildings is an intrinsic part of the non-verbal world. It adds dimension to our lives and this acts as an extension to human body communication and provides a comfortable environment which enhances our feelings of well-being. Our verbal and non-verbal communication will be more positive as a result of our comfort with our environment.

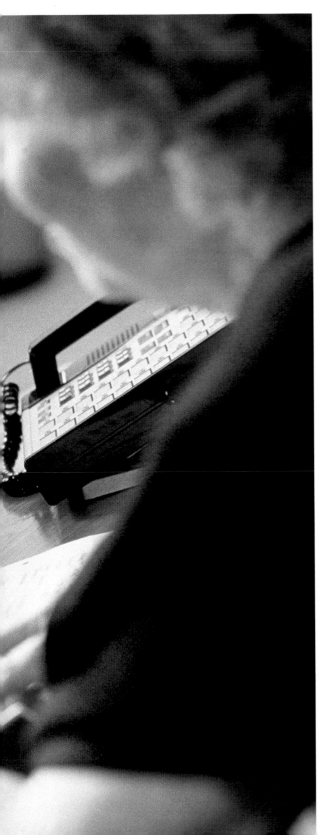

LEFT: This meeting seems to be going well. The man has an open, friendly manner. This allows the woman to relax and express herself freely. His body language is not negative which would create a barrier between the two that might result in an aggressive atmosphere, hostile exchange or even stunt the flow of conversation.

Cultural Differences

As we mentioned earlier, some body language is innate and is shared by the whole of humanity, whereas other forms are cultural and are learned. With this latter form, we have to be particularly careful when visiting a foreign country, since misunderstandings can arise and create the potential for conflict.

RIGHT: Beware! You are entering my territory, go no further. We might use this common gesture in a number of ways, and in a number of professions.

For instance, the sign we commonly know as the "OK" sign – where the thumb and forefinger are made into an "O" – is seen as vulgar in Turkey. Equally in France the same gesture means "zero". The cultural interpretations can really cause problems in Brazil, where the gesture is a sexual insult.

The simple act of raising your hand to stop a man in Greece is one of the gravest insults you could throw there. You have just inadvertently said that you would like to sleep with one of his female relatives in five different positions. This may be a coarse example, but it illustrates the hazards of being ignorant of gestural inferences outside your own culture.

Many Pakistani and Indian nationals shake their head when they are agreeing with something you are saying. By simply putting your hands on your hips in some of the Pacific Rim countries you are expressing anger. By showing the sole of your foot in some Arab societies you are insulting them. In Arab countries generally it is extremely impolite to touch a female to whom you are not related.

In the West we commonly touch our children on the head as a greeting or to show affection. In the Far East this can offend religious sensibilities. Likewise kissing is regarded very differently around the world and indeed a whole book could be written on this subject alone.

LEFT: Hands on hips can be interpreted in different ways. In some instances they have an underlying sexual message. The arms and hands form a triangle that points to the genitalia. This gesture can also indicate stubbornness when allied with stern facial gestures.

There remain some cultures which do not engage in the kiss, notably Papuans, the Balinese and certain African peoples who prefer to rub noses or suck each other's mouth with an inhaling action. Western influences continue to spread, however, and even these peoples are increasingly adopting our own modes of body language, particularly in the younger and less traditional generations.

In the West the kiss is a sign of affection. In much of Eastern Asia the kiss is inappropriate outside the bedroom, and it still offends older Chinese and Japanese today when they spot teenagers kissing in public. A kiss with the opposite sex on the streets of Kuwait will land you in trouble.

When travelling abroad – particularly in less liberal countries – be advised that strong and emotive uses of body language are likely to offend. If in doubt watch the local people. See how they use space, observe what gestures they employ and remember to utilise the same rules yourself.

If you are crossing a border then you will need to be very aware of what messages you are sending out, particularly non-verbal ones. It will be more than likely that you cannot speak the language and thus your only means of communication will be by gestures. Avoid at all cost getting into a confrontation or gesticulating wildly.

As a general rule, minimise all your conscious body language until you are sure of the messages that will be conveyed. At first, stick with the kind of body language that we all understand – smiles, attentiveness, and the showing of a positive attitude through your physical reactions. Remember that while gestures are often culturally determined, good manners are universal and you can show these very simply through polite non-verbal behaviour.

ABOVE: The handshake is a common Western gesture that has multiple functions, including introducing oneself for the first time, sealing a financial deal, or saying a formal goodbye.

OPPOSITE: Embracing is a sign of mutual love and friendship with those that are close to us. However public displays of affection can cause offense in some countries.

Clothing and Appearance

People will often make informed and accurate decisions about you purely by assessing your clothes and appearance. They will deduce information about your wealth, status and occupation. Just look how many magazine racks are given over to titles that deal purely with our appearance.

BELOW: Open body language and an eye for one's appearance are crucial factors when entering a job interview.

Appearances are culturally and geographically determined. The more permissive societies allow people to make all sorts of statements about themselves ranging from displays of power to sexual invitations. We dress for confidence; to massage our egos; to send a physical signal to somebody that we want a job and have presented ourselves accordingly.

Our appearance is meticulously scrutinised by the people we see around us. Every physical feature from the size of our chest, the length of our hair, our waistline, even the size of our shirt collar is essentially a non-verbal piece of communication that an observer will sift and sort through, mostly subconsciously; hence fat people are seen to be jolly and genial, thin people introverted and nervous. People who wear business suits are judged as being competent, whereas people who wear blazers are considered to be conservative. Much of this stereotyping is often quite damaging as it gives no account of the real individual beneath the clothes, but nevertheless it is part of our collective psychology and cannot be ignored.

ABOVE: The business suit and tie remain the standard dress for the corporate world. More creative businesses, such as advertising houses, strive for a more avant-garde or casual dress code to distinguish themselves from their competition.

The Business Suit

The best-dressed people are the ones who catch our eye. They not only epitomise smartness and poise, but exude messages about their own personality, independence and even their sexuality.

In the business world the well-cut suit is associated with high status and relative wealth. Men and women who dress in dark suits are perceived to be ambitious and socially motivated.

The suit remains very much the "uniform" of the business world, with a few exceptions made for creative enterprises like advertising and design, where individuality is encouraged.

We very often identify the colours of clothes with certain professions. Thus we may very well imagine the man completely dressed in black is an undertaker. Greys, greens and navy blues give a formal and serious look, with navy blue projecting an image of dignity. It is rare to see red in hospitals; rather blues and whites and similar "caring" hues are adopted as uniform to instil a feeling of well-being in patients and relatives alike.

"Power dressing" is far from exclusively a male trait where appearance is concerned. With so many more women of high-ranking positions in the business world, the female business suit is now a common sight. There are however some difficulties to transcend where the female business suit is concerned. Do you for instance cover the neck up? The exposed female neck is a sexually alluring feature to many males. A dress that accentuates the cleavage may well distract a male counterpart. High-heeled shoes again enhance the sway of the buttocks and the chest of the woman. Are these attributes quite the right ones to show in the business world? Many such questions are down to each woman's individual taste. For both sexes, the business suit has evolved into a piece of cunningly crafted cloth that states unequivocally: "I am a model of efficiency, power and formality." The necktie is used to conceal the neck as this feature of the body is perceived as an area of vulnerability.

In a different scenario, by simply donning a pair of jeans you are making a completely opposing statement of body language. A pair of jeans is popularly supposed to signal rebellion. In a different scenario, the epaulettes on a military uniform serve no other purpose than to make the shoulders of the wearer more impressive. Again they are indicators of power, status and rank.

A skinhead is often perceived as threatening; a non-conformist because he does not apply the same set of rules to appearance as the majority of us do.

We have a set of rules about our appearances and anybody that chooses to breach them is judged accordingly. Thus a man with "I love Mum" tattooed on his forehead might be sending us all an endearing message about his relationship with his mother, but many of us are unlikely to want to socialise with him since the tattoo also tells us that he is a misfit in society.

In a multitude of ways, then, clothes and general appearance influence our perception of others. This illustrates how body language works all the time – from the moment we show ourselves in public when we leave our homes in the morning, and every second of the day.

OPPOSITE: The man in the tie looks businesslike and prepared for the next task. His posture suggests a positive approach. His counterpart however is more casual in appearance and posture, demonstrated by the way he is slouching.

LEFT: While the manager is dictating letters, he maintains a relaxed and confident body posture toward his secretary. This in turn relaxes her, as can be seen in the confident eye contact and attentiveness to his words as she writes.

Parents and Children

Body language plays an increasingly important role in our formative years. These early years are a critical stage in the development of relationships between parents and their offspring. On the face of it, most of the signals we send to each other might seem quite trivial. A baby cries because it is hungry. It smiles because it is happy. We respond accordingly. Mothers in particular are inherently adept at conveying the correct body language to their children, whatever the child's age.

BELOW: Touching is a vital ingredient of body language that helps a developing child understand that it is loved and wanted.

Our earliest sensations are of dark and yet safe suspension in the womb; sensations of warmth, comfort and overall security. Then all of a sudden the walls come crashing down on that safe world. We are forced from our home of nine months or so, into a clinical world of dazzling lights, strange shapes and alien smells. The placenta is cut and we immediately seek bodily contact with our mother.

From this point on body language becomes important. For the mother this will involve all manners of embrace, rocking to and fro, lip contact with the infant's head. All these are vital cornerstones for attachments that we will develop as we become older.

Should this process of developing body language be interrupted or denied, then there will almost certainly be repercussions later on in life. Within a few months babies learn how to smile; they use the smile as a signalling device to their parents. Those endearing smiles are perhaps the most original and positive messages they can transmit to their parents. The ways in which the parents react to these signals and others form the basis for determining the child's future

ABOVE: Small children often hold their hands up "automatically" to tell their parents non-verbally that they want physical contact and the ensuing comfort that comes from it.

development. Children left to cry interminably in the initial few months of life, their signals falling on deaf ears, will very likely grow up maladjusted. They will have difficulties in forming relationships because they still bear the psychological scars. They will not have learned how to communicate effectively with appropriate body language, and research suggests that this cannot be learned effectively later in life.

As an individual matures, he or she will learn a new set of body language rules appropriate for use amongst his peer group. Young children will learn these through play, and teenagers will copy the mannerisms of their role models at school and on TV. Body language is most readily learned through the development of close friendships and relationships. As such it is an ongoing process which lasts throughout life.

BELOW: The reassuring hug that child and parent alike need from time to time.

LEFT: Learn to recognise the gestures and postures of a withdrawn or sulking child; by doing so you can learn to defuse any conflict before it arrives.

Summing up

Body language which projects feelings of warmth, security, concern, parity and a willingness to cooperate with others should be your aim. Body language which conveys inappropriate messages – or is simply lacking in positivity – is bound to lead to discord.

OPPOSITE: Three dissimilar reactions at a party. The woman on the far left is quite at ease with her surroundings, whereas to her left her friend seems slightly rigid but nevertheless still conveys warmth. The seated woman however, bears all the hallmarks of being reserved, reflected in her crossed arms and legs.

We need to learn how to display a balanced view of ourselves when using body language. What does a blank face tell our employer, or our lover? The message is, surprisingly, fundamentally the same: "I am emotionless, I feel neutral about this." Most relationships in life demand commitment, not neutrality. You have to make a conscious effort to ensure that your body language conveys positivity.

In many ways, verbal communication is an artificial and remote language. To be truly effective the voice needs to combine with our visual and tactile behaviour. The blend of all three then gives the language the resonance and accessibility required by others to understand us and the feelings we are trying to convey.

Our written language becomes incommunicable and largely unintelligible if we remove the punctuation. It becomes merely an endless stream of monotonous information. By adding the exclamation marks, commas and full stops we give it vibrancy and colour. Try then to think of your body language in this way. What signal are you sending to others if you remove all that punctuation? Somebody with a blank facial countenance may be sending a message that is equally blank. Similarly someone with a fixed smile will look equally out of place.

Try to be more direct in everything you do, from your eye contact to letting somebody know exactly how you feel about a situation. If you feel hurt then tell people; similarly if you admire somebody then tell them. Body language in a sense should be a series of actions which expresses your opinions and emotions but makes no outright demands on others.

RIGHT: This couple seem to have established a good rapport. Close body positioning, strong eye contact, and her leaning on her arm as she listens to him all reflect intense interest in each other.

An individual who is observed to be relaxed in posture, his arms relaxed, his facial features steady, who maintains eye contact, who smiles, nods and talks with his hands and who recognises how to use the space around him ultimately has a positive effect on us. The same individual who makes sudden movements, looks at the floor, touches himself excessively, adopts stiff postures and whose eyelids are blinking rapidly will be seen in a negative light.

There are many obvious signs that can help us to determine the state of mind of another. Staring down at the floor tends to send signals of apprehension, guilt, shame and even fear. If a person denies doing something and then instinctively levels his gaze to the floor then this is a good example of body language not supporting the vocal communication. This instantly raises doubts in our minds about their sincerity.

Nervous scratching and eye rubbing are negative aspects of body language that need to be erased from our repertoire, and replaced with laughing, smiling and sincere tones of voice.

We need to be constantly aware of even the slightest actions which may influence our understanding of someone. Thus a person we see biting his lips is telling us he is angry. If we can spot this then we can act accordingly to get to the root of his anger. Recognise all those yawns, lowered brows, frowns and superior tones of voice for what they are and you will at once have a larger and more vivid picture of what the person is telling you about himself.

LEFT: Body and eye contact help to establish the bonds between couples that can last a lifetime.

ABOVE: Whether we like it or not, what we wear conveys to others certain information, which may be accurate, or simply assumptions on their part.

Conclusion

To come to a satisfactory conclusion on how to use and interpret body language more effectively, we have to regard it in its entirety. We can easily draw erroneous and sometimes dangerous conclusions by trying to interpret a single non-verbal sign, when we should in fact be observing the dynamics of the whole body. We don't read half a sentence of written text and draw a conclusion from it, and the same rule applies with interpreting body language.

At first it may seem a bit of an alien concept to open your palms or maintain eye contact with somebody when you have been used to hiding your hands behind your back and only looking briefly into someone else's eyes. But as you become consciously aware of doing this more and seeing others do the same you will begin to feel far more comfortable about yourself; as your own self-esteem rises then you transfer this directly to the other person.

Learn to recognise the qualities you can bring to a social interaction by presenting a fuller and rounder image of yourself. Focus on sending positive messages about yourself and you will soon see a change in the way others perceive you, treat you and cooperate with you. Try and identify any areas in your body language that might be distracting or discouraging others to interact with you fully. Why isn't that person maintaining eye contact with you? Is it because you are not maintaining it with them? Perhaps it is because they are nervous of you.

Body language should always be in harmony with what is being said. Each should complement the other; if there is conflict between them then there is every chance that falsities are being said. It should underline what you say and do, not undermine it. An example of an instance where the two do not match up is with "false friendliness". As we all know, this is usually easily identifiable and has very negative results.

Try to piece together all the individual gestures and non-verbal responses that we have discussed and use them as one fluent language; think about the proximity to a person you have when interacting. Are you using the space well? Would the other person feel more comfortable if you moved forward one more step, or would they feel threatened? Are you right to increase your interaction at this moment or would it be better to wait for another time?

Gauge your eye contact so that you are looking at the other person for at least 60 per cent of the conversation; smile more frequently; nod when you are interested and when you want somebody to know you understand them; relax your posture and lean forwards slightly; adopt an open body with no barriers such as crossed arms or hands in pockets; pay attention to your grooming. Think also about your tone of voice, how much volume you need to project it successfully, and the pace at which you are delivering it. People respond more positively to accessible and well enunciated speech than they do to a garbled, breathless message. Aim then for a clear and audible voice that sends a concise message to the listener. Regulate your breathing.

Think of body language as a code that has to be decoded by your opposite number. The more enigmatic you make your code the less chance that person has of decoding it successfully. Recognise the use of touch in the right circumstances and how effective it can be to signify support for somebody.

Consider the environment you are in. Is a dimly lit factory full of noisy machinery the best place to discuss a personal problem with a work colleague? Consider also any cultural differences, particularly regarding strangers. Respect other people's territories and their own privacy just as you would expect them to respect yours.

Be more open about yourself and let others know how you actually feel about something or someone. Have a sense of direction when you are next interacting with somebody and avoid at all costs character assassination, putting other people down, sarcasm and prurience. By eliminating these things you will find that people will see in you a different person to the one they thought they knew. By learning to stand up for yourself more and communicating with others more efficiently, you are opening up a whole new world for yourself. You now have the ability to influence those around you, rather than being the object of other people's manipulation. Body language has empowered you.

BELOW: This couple are clearly comfortable with each other's use of space. Recognising the importance of using proximity in everyday situations helps us to get a better feel for the verbal communication that follows.

INDEX

The publishers would like to thank the following sources for their kind permission to reproduce the pictures in this book:

Allsport (U.K.) Ltd/David Rogers 15
Corbis/Owen Franken 49
Carlton Books Ltd./Sue Atkinson 7, 10r, 16, 18-25, 27, 28, 29, 30, 31, 34-47, 50-58, 63-70, 76, 77, 79, 81-83, 88-91, 93
The Image Bank 62l/Barros & Barros 12-13
Pictorial Press Ltd. 14 l, 17
Rex Features/John Powell 73/Tim Rooke 26
Tony Stone Images/Bruce Ayres 62br, 72, 74/Joe Cornish 85/Tim Davis 11tl/Dale Durfee 78/Howie Garber 10 l/Howard Grey 71/Eric Larrayadieu 87/Renee Lynn 11b/Dennis O'Clair 84/Lee Page 60-61/Joe Polillio 94/Tamara Reynolds 8-9/Jon Riley 32-33/Bob Thomas 14tr/Penny Tweedie 59/John Warden 11tr/Jennie Woodcock 86